A growing list of your author's books
are attached in the back of this book
for your inspection.

Offsetting Climate Change

And

Resolving The Nuclear Waste Contamination

Lloyd E. McIlveen

Order this book online at www.trafford.com
or email orders@trafford.com

Most Trafford titles are also available at major online book retailers.

Print information available on the last page.

ISBN: 978-1-4907-0519-4 (sc)
ISBN: 978-1-4907-0518-7 (e)

Library of Congress Control Number: 2013913722

Trafford rev. 04/08/2016

 www.trafford.com

North America & international
toll-free: 1 888 232 4444 (USA & Canada)
fax: 812 355 4082

This book is offered to the public as an instrument toward offsetting major or cataclysmic chaos which climate change and nuclear waste contamination has created and is presented as an example of ideas and ideals that may be helpful in furthering the cause of survival for all the world's living beings on the surface of the planet.

The contents of this book are also submitted as seeds to be nourished for the mature growth, containment and advancement of living standards on this very unique planet we call Earth for the benefit of its successful future.

Actually, the term climate change originated from the term global warming which was only a precursor description of what will unfold around the globe.

We are now learning more of our sooner than later future.

Introduction

The readers of this book on impending calamity certainly do reserve the right to suggest the author of this type of prophesying and promoting is attempting to negate optimistic outlooks and display negative vibrations of and for the future of mankind. If that's the case, it would behoove those readers to alternate a little in perspective toward possibilities and indicating another view may shed light on this subject of climate change of which is frighteningly starring at us right in the face with its intent to annihilate mankind.

Is climate change and nuclear contamination a matter of true or false? How about maybe or maybe not? Can we be absolute about anything?

Some things "are" positive and some things "are" negative, but either are only a matter of how one views it.

Sufficient evidence in interpretation certainly helps when it pertains to analyzing this world condition.

This author chooses prevention and preparing methods and also claims, at least at this point, the methods within these scriptures are a form of positivity as compared to "letting it all happen as it may." Nothing meaningful has ever happened when one sits by the wayside with hopes and beliefs only.

Some of the readers may reach a foregoing conclusion concerning these contents either at the beginning, the middle or the end and chose to assail the following scripts as a form of negative assertions. If that's the case, they must take heed to that famous old question, "What if you're wrong?"

Let us proceed with a positive "and" negative approach. Everything and anything "does" exist with both. Both are those of which are comprised of the basics of movement and thought. Let us discover the positives, negatives, ifs ands or buts and the reals from the unreals, if you will, of a lurking and still controversial situation among certain groups. It deserves serious probing at this time for survival purposes as will be described in the following chapters.

This is a time when we all need to read, probe, sort out public information and think in alike terms more than ever if we want to prevent, preserve and maintain an alive population on planet Earth for our future. That future is being threatened by an atmosphere drying out phenomenon.

There is plenty of ocean which isn't much of a threat beside tsunamis, rising seas and dying salt water animals, but fresh water will soon accelerate in process of elimination via climate change and other extreme temperature changes related with accompanying natural disasters in reaction to the temperature changes.

Our major concern now is to gain more knowledge of the oncoming function of disaster for getting serious about stopping this monstrous threat we have brought unto ourselves; all of us.

The following chapters will describe general and detailed urgencies for seriously dealing with this life threatening dilemma. Along with that, the issue of resolving the nuclear waste problem will be displayed for solutions to change the present threat.

Preface

Solving, resolving and offsetting climate change and eliminating nuclear waste storage is what it's about.

Water consciousness has existed among humans, animals and insects etc. for many millenniums. Over a lengthily period of time, there has been either too much water such as melting icebergs and snow etc. or rain and some proverbs claim a completely flooded earth. The scientific and religious views we have commonly known offer perspective for evaluating these possible realities.

Sure, in the lifetime of humans, many areas have been the interim exception. However, over the vast period of Earth's existence, ancient history has revealed massive fires and drouts occurring which have resulted in different forms of deterioration than drouts.

Recent centuries alone have unveiled vast areas of forest left baron from human development projects let alone the natural disasters around the globe which have reduced vegetation to bald land over that longer period of time which has contributed toward precipitation reduction.

Long term views of planet Earth's history reveals everything cycles from one vast era to another and therefore becomes normal and natural. Who are "we" to deal with the almost inconceivable turn of natural events over millions or billions of years? Only the forces and influences of nature or God, whichever one chooses the most to believe, can swing a deal to completely change what mankind can only experience. However, mankind does contribute.

Climate change and nuclear waste disposal is contaminating our environment and needs our responsible attention.

So what? Who cares what has happened or could? Even though mankind, up to and around the twentieth century, didn't pay much heed to the creeping and oncoming dilemma that would in one way or another affect our way of life; we can, to a meaningful extent, assist nature in preventing grossly disastrous affects to humans, animals and others.

The present rate of progress, in at least altering the fresh water diminishing situation of which mankind has contributed, is far short of meeting the demands of survival in a modern and technological society of people. They are not only accelerating the population growth unchecked, but most indications display unwillingness to alter that destiny. When the water is gone, we will be gone.

Lagging behind, contentions dealing with reality can easily state the near term population will diminish and die before the next weather cycle occurs if attention to correcting this inevitable climate change, water diminishing and nuclear waste disposal situation isn't seriously addressed, tackled and offset.

The world and all its living creatures can dry up or burn up and become a planet such as Mars or so many others which appear lifeless. This can happen through ignoring the option of prevention methods. Yes, prevention methods generally work if accepted objectively, planned carefully and promoted with the intent of changing an obvious deteriorating environment.

The water, warming and waste problem "can" be solved, resolved and corrected in greater part than less and it may begin to materialize right here in the analyzation of these scripts. That is the intention in these scripts; to be instrumental in gaining attention to this past and more recently important issue for the survival of mankind and their wild counterparts on planet Earth and maintain an improved standard of existence.

Again, so what? It is said disasters have always lingered and hit living beings while the remainders seem to survive. Well, would you want your family to be the one's who didn't survive?

It's different now. World population has never been so vast. This is something we have to deal with, however, for quite some time. Philosophically and humanely, it's a worse case scenario for billions of people to suffer debilitating, excruciating and unnecessary misery in the dieing process than it was for, let's say, a few hundred thousand years ago when the world's societies of people began; at least so it goes with the scientific theory of deduction in history.

The content of this book reveals inevitable disasters pertaining to inadequate water availability in combating climate change and nuclear waste contamination. The book also deals with how to offset those inevitabilities through analysis, planned capabilities and approach.

The beginning segments in description, prior to planning and approach, describes the water/dryness dilemma in perspective so understanding the solution will wave the anxiety of which many times leads to hasty and unwise decisions in evaluating a course of cure to follow or lead.

Severity of the existing problem is gradually described from cause and effect into creative efforts of solving the problem for a workable solution and may be accepted for reinstating the temperature and tranquility of our original environment.

If science doesn't solve the problems soon, there are only two choices left. One is to reverse population growth immediately that is creating warming and contaminating conditions or initiate a method of offsetting the inevitable scorcher.

Workable methods to offset the problems are offered in these scripts. World governments are too slow. Their agendas are too lengthy, under funded and not realistically serious enough for cooperatively and coordinatively rallying many nations together for this necessary cause of which will require our world's people to follow suit. So what has to happen?

There are only two societal segments on the globe who can handle that task; the governments of the world or the people of the world. That's it! If the governments aren't able or even qualified as a power of one, then like it's been said, we the people must initiate the project. This will be explained in the chapters ahead and more in your author's "Preventing The Doom Of Mankind" on the list in back as time passes. This printing is 2014.

Contents

Chapter 1

Why worry about water now? Cause and effect

Everything concerning water is pretty much status quo on planet Earth at the present time unless it is in reference to starving and thirst laden countries such as nations of Africa, some islands on the planet and what will happen to all Earth's inhabitants in time at the present rate of climate change etc.

Most humans refrain from taking action on threatening situations until the threats become real happenings and are placed right in their laps.

Some people remember the trigger of World War II when it was called a sneak attack. Poppycock! Some of those folks also remember there was plenty of evidence ahead of a major attack. The U.S. just didn't want to confront the possibility and do anything about it. They kept their heads smugly and snugly in their covered holes like rabbits hoping nothing would really expose them to, as they now say, harms way.

The attack on Pearl Harbor is only one example of societies of the entire world relaxing in states of fantasy especially when they have suffered and apparently recovered from previous major encounters. It seems the nature of the beast to relax after a feast or famine is complimented by the urge to ignore.

Wars, per se, are an effect of discontent or greed. Saying there will always be disastrous effects following discontent or greed may appear fairly harsh, hard, obtruse and/or limited in scope, but much has and is being learned by these inequitable appearing incidents.

Mankind may not be ready yet to efficiently discourage the path of a large asteroid heading toward planet Earth, but our species of living beings do possess the capability of developing earthly systems that can change the unfolding course of inevitable consequences such as the potential for planet Earth to dry up as what may have happened to planet Mars. Who cares now? We don't live that long? It won't be in "our" life time, you say? Think a little more!

The water calamity may not occur severally in present day generations, but the possibility of it happening at a continuously accelerating rate into following generations must be seriously considered for their sake and yes, for the future of mankind or at least any future that we can imagine. Momentum can shockingly accelerate!

Consider the world population expansion. It is very seriously being ignored and overlooked. It doesn't take a physicist to multiply the present rate of expansion times time to determine the amount of people who will cover the earth in a relatively short period of time along with the needs and greeds they subliminally acquired. Let us prepare "before" it happens.

The more people there are, after too many, the more general resources and water degradation will occur accompanied by nature's toll of change. The combination of the two may result in an early death of a planet's species of living beings.

What "is" the cause for the effect? It isn't only overzeal, overconsumption and greed particularly. The cause is partially due to planet Earth's original and basic makeup in the formation of the planet which was a fury of combustible components, gases and moisture. While that spectacular flourished, this particular planet experienced a battle of the elements prior to the settling of the earth that formed the sphere we now term as Earth. The potential for fire and water apparently was designed, if you will, to be compatible with the tolerances of living beings, at least on Earth, since there is no evidence of these protoplasmic characters existing anywhere in "our" solar system.

However, it also seems the forces of nature have always stuck to a code of its own in worldly changes.

The early days of formation featured only one leader which was nature, however it is perceived. Currently, there are two front runners; nature and man. Most appearances indicate mankind is now a front runner in changing, or at least attempting to change, the destination and disposition of fire and water. There has always been waste contamination of some kind. Mankind is just condensing, spreading or rearranging it for what they believe is "their" advantage. A variation of their original beliefs are beginning to appear on the horizon of progress. They, as a whole and advanced society, are beginning to realize humanity and their progress must blend in an equilibrium suited for the compatibility of the two.

There is, needless to say, plenty of water on the surface of this planet, but a great part of it isn't practically useful, except for power, especially as it is obviously being contaminated by mankind's soaring waste problem.

Now, there is the nuclear waste nuisance. Nuclear power, which covers a multitude of services, is basically clean. It's just the waste material that makes it contaminating and unacceptable. The plan in these texts is one of which will eliminate waste material without the necessity of burying it in the earth or in the mountains.

Nuclear power is becoming and will be a necessary alternative source and way of life of the future for running the industry of power. The production of nuclear bombs, not withstanding their potency, isn't near the ongoing threat as climate change and will only be elaborated on as a source of nuclear waste to be dealt with. Nuclear war is completely another story.

Given and applying the essential methods and "tools" for eliminating those waste materials, mankind will create a clean, safe and more useable source of power.

Burying nuclear waste in the ground will eventually eat its way into the earth's soil and atmosphere; then cause more essential elements preserving water to burn which will contribute toward higher temperatures hence, further deteriorating of living species.

Would you believe Grand Canyon, among other notable rivers, canyons and gorges, was many times higher and/or deeper at one or more times much before living beings arrived on Earth? Think about it! That condition remained as such for millions of years.

Now, all that useable moister is diminishing at a beyond normal acceleration in large by climate change plus population consumption and abuse. This is world wide. Look at the highest mountain in Africa; Mt. Kilimanjaro. The snow peak (fresh water) is disappearing faster than they can estimate. That's nature and mankind doing their thing!

When more people gather, more fresh water is needed and more fires occur, generally. The U.S. is experiencing that dilemma now especially in the dryer lands of forests, lower tree/brush and other areas having been originally covered with plush vegetation.

When the lands become dry by nature, an issue doesn't seem to be made of it. When the land becomes dry because of mankind's overpopulation, consumption and abuse, more of something eventually is needed to squelch or offset those dilemmas.

The experts and official fire combatants are admitting the battle to win over raging fires in this era of time isn't happening. It is such where we can only do our best. Some call it trying.

The forests are being stripped by mankind with insufficient vegetation replacement.

Massive trees contribute toward rain. Precipitation is drastically reducing in those baron lands. There just isn't enough water to substantially regrow those areas. Water, trees and rain helps in keeping the earth's surface cool. The globe's surface "is" warming! Technically speaking, fresh water "is" beginning to dry up!

The people of planet Earth must understand better what has been occurring on the surface of the earth: The nucleus of the earth (center of the earth) is normally the hottest area. The temperature is lessoned as it reaches the surface of the earth. The temperature outward from the earth becomes colder. The atmospheric pressure isn't enough to keep the earth cool enough for life against the vulnerability of heat penetrating through the layers of earth's surface where oil was once abundant to insulate its surface.

The oil extracted for the past hundred and fifty years or so has also robbed the crust of the earth of a vital cooling source. The heat from cars, trucks, planes, war, trains and even spacecraft lifting off the ground certainly hasn't helped the situation.

The oil "is" on its way toward depletion levels, but in the meantime, those cavities in the earth are absorbing heat from below. That heat radiates through to the surface and adds to caloric imbalance in temperature. It all adds to the climate change dilemma.

So, the cause is a combination of nature resisting man's irresponsible dispositioning of nature's basic fire, water, earth and air.

There "is" a way to win the battle and retain our caloric/moisture equilibrium fairly close to what nature may have intended.

The term "nature" in these scripts is meant to express that of a maker or maintainer of all existence; but is not necessarily a conventional view of deity. The express creed here is as follows: Everything in all the universes are a specific design created by a source of intelligence of which mankind hasn't yet been informed and is apparently meant to be as it is. An exception to that philosophy may be when mankind's flowing results of cooperation indicate those changes blend with the mentioned realm of nature.

This world of civilization has all indications they will burn and dry up without exercising some type of solution to offset it.

Solving and resolving for candid solutions to these stated and ongoing threats will continue throughout the chapters in a manner designed to attract and spread attention to and from everyone possible.

Tendencies, as we go, are to remind the readers to retain what has been stated for the benefit of focusing in on a final decision to or not to accept the descriptions, contentions, proposals and solutions offered.

This is about our health, sanity and existence of present and future humanity. It's at stake now. Everything will not be peachy keen in our near future at the present rate.

Chapter 2

Diminishing and unusable water is not the "only" hindrance to mankind's survival

The problem with the problem is it's not just one problem of water we have to deal with. They "are" working at a creeping pace of speed to filter sea water for human consumption. There "is" plenty of it. It might be quicker though, to design a method for our stomachs to digest the salt and debris than changing the massive tonnage of sea water. This, of course, is pure speculation at present.

The fires mentioned in chapter one are largely contributing factors toward the threat to our survival. The forests are burning down somewhat unchecked at present and at this point in time, there is nothing immediately effective enough to fully conquer "that" dilemma. Most buildings are built with wood and they are burning down at a somewhat alarming rate. Sure, a portion of it is from arsenists. The rest of it is from carelessness, explosions, lightning and of course, faulty or displaced wiring, chemicals or grease etc. Wind is also a big factor in widespread fires. Most of these types of fires requires, detrimentally, tapping into our standard water supply wherever it is to saturate the fires.

While this persistent fire threat hovers at the present rate of acceleration along with borrowing water from other areas, it will only last so long; it won't cure the fire problem. So, which is worse, the fire problem or the water problem?

Again, the population is growing at an unchecked rate. That means double, triple, quadruple or more of everything will be needed. Every time there is a need of some kind, there is energy expended in the process of distributing that energy to the need. All energy expended is a form of heat. That's a lot of heat in view it is increasing, not decreasing and that heat is tapping the relative and ambient temperatures of the world on the outside and penetrating the surface of the earth along with the natural rising heat from within the earth.

Little by little, everything in the area of energy output for utility and industrial purposes is going electrical. Eventually, the electrostatic, electromagnetic and electrokinetic work intertwining that increased power may decrease the efficiency of power and negate theories of man-made power thereby transforming an earthly disturbance of which may not only trigger a release of gravity, but may cause fires or explosions in the growing amount of nuclear power plants spreading more heat related chaos around the globe. That example may seem a little unreal at present, however, similar situations do not need a trigger mechanism. Heat causes pressure and pressure causes heat. The result can be unplanned disasters of multiple proportion requiring unknown gobs of water to douse it.

The less evenly distributed water with all this chaos, the more damage can occur to the inhabitants. General and unbelievable chaos similarly mentioned in your author's book "The Paradox of Progress Unfolding 1" can imaginatively unfold on planet Earth or something very similar.

Many times, imagination evolves into reality. Let us not tempt these possibilities.

Making matters appear even worse is the factor where disease of all natures can occur when a problem of these mentioned magnitudes is not seriously addressed, approached, solved, resolved and corrected; at least to some degree.

Whenever and wherever nations waiver their instincts, stance and rights to prevent disease and chaos, their standards diminish to a poverty and vulnerable state.

Technically and realistically, we of the whole planet are slowly intering an era of becoming an extinct species of beings by not creating enough useable initiatives for preventing or at least altering the oncoming chaos not particularly of nuclear war, but of the everyday situations we of mankind do create such as ozone suffication, fires, overpopulation, the water problem and disease either self-inflected or indirectly imposed by ignorance, greed, deception or unwillingness to extend effort or surrender anything gained for an important cause such as contributing to the cause of mankind's survival and better health standards.

What does all this have to do with resolving the water problem? Any problem that escapes coherency and stability doesn't begin or progress on it's own merits or one reason. It exists, forms and grows as a result of many contributing factors. All the factors mentioned in these chapters contribute toward the deteriorating or dry up process of mankind and probably all other living beings too; especially when all those who are recipients of the impending disaster turn their heads and pass the buck, if you will, in the direction of someone else to worry about.

We are all getting to the time when it's necessary for everyone to gain survival consciousness in a technological time of accelerating progress.

If everyone or at least an amount sufficient to do the job, would join in efforts to support and/or promote an adaptable solution that will eventually be revealed in these scripts, the disease from chaos perpetrated by insufficient water will be curtailed and offset or slowly reversed for a comfortable and foreseeable time.

Survival of all living beings is threatened by fire and suffication due to conditions previously mentioned.

Although many may object and disagree by virtue of a holy spirit concept, the destiny of all living species is presently at risk of perishing because of an inability to physically adapt to present and near future atmospheric temperature and humidity causing protoplasmic deterioration in living beings.

When and if mankind ignores these realistic possibilities, an ill fated and mental state of mind can rule the roost where they may not adapt to preventive measures and will become victims of their own metamorphic transformation into an oblivious end.

An obliviously uncontrolled end is a worse case scenario and certainly not absolute because anything can change as time passes. Surprises of all natures have always rained from the heavens, so to speak.

However, if the preceding scenario applies, it's time to start recognizing the signs and begin preparations for making changes and additions in water objectives.

If we are truly entering into a new ice age of twelve to fifteen thousand years, the water problem may not be so intense or even exist at all. A supporting agreement may state humans may not survive through it anyway. When there are no humans, there is no contamination.

However, another contention favoring the nonsurvival aspect may state an overpopulated and highly technological earth will burn its way through the ice and snow and return back to the water chaos situation even much quicker than the previous ice age with an inexplicably worse problem. Nature must prevail.

Regardless of evolutionary change in the time of the future, we have to deal with conditions relative to the time of our lives and of our immediate and close term families, right? All of that depends on how eternally and internally philosophical our mind's function. We can support the cause of prevention or only give a hoot about today as though now is all there is.

If people can exonerate themselves from belief and exploitation indoctrination for awhile, they can view and more efficiently understand how they think and feel concerning the possibility of taking a stand on supporting and promoting the water preservation initiative manner of approach. This will all be elaborated on chronologically in the following chapters.

This book "is" an initiative of which deals with changing or altering mankind's destiny by virtue of utilizing the birthright of choice to engage in objective decisions which may require voting depending on how a segment of each country along with the main committee decides to handle the whole project. Whether it is managed by the governments or private enterprise, the people's support is still needed for best results.

What to do about the elimination of nuclear waste will follow in the order it is planned. Thank you for being patient because that is exactly what is needed for comprehensively understanding the global perspective and consciousness of this most important issue at stake; gathering the world's people together for supporting the cause of offsetting climate change and eliminating nuclear waste materials so we and future generations can live without being choked to death by heat and intoxicating air.

There is a possibility of climate change variations and reactions where extreme earthquakes, hurricanes, floods and other phenomenal earthly functions will occur as temperature change side effects and will wipe out millions of people to say the least. That is good for reducing the population, but what if it's you and/or your family members or their offsprings?

Living on a crumbling planet with no one anymore won't exactly be a "happiness is a family affair" while tumbling around and being battered from one man-made disaster to another searching for fresh water to barely survive. What a slow, miserable way to die and no one to help because they are also being tossed around. That may all sound like a science/fiction drama from a much in demand movie from people who desire extreme entertainment, but in not too long of a time, we could be the true life actors and actresses of the "end of mankind dilemma" with no one surviving if we, all of us, continue to ignore those possibilities of which can very easily become probabilities through not enough people accepting responsibility for saving us. We are leading up to "more" reality as we move through the chapters.

Chapter 3

First things must come first, as always, in any plan. Getting the attention of people and politicians is first

The water problem is already underway. Mankind has grown too big and fast for their britches and has outgrown their old fashioned simplicity. They are now running immaterially wild in their pursuit to grow everything. True, success is dependent on growth, but not accelerated overgrowth of which has and is occurring practically unchecked.

The need for containing and regulating growth must happen first in the line of priorities concerning raising "children of progress." We never really grow up. We just keep reaching up and out for more and it gets out of hand as is fairly obvious.

Next in line of priorities is maintaining a consistent awareness of the problem so as to, number three in priorities, display it to others; particularly to others in position of authority so they may extrapolate the details and necessities to their staffs for more evaluation and decision making efforts.

So, viewing the problem, we are running out of water for large scale public and private uses around the world. These uses will be described in the next chapter.

Increasing an awareness where #1, we take these water uses for granted and #2, when we have them doesn't really allow us to keep them or #3, even our survival until #4. it may be too late has to prompt us into action of #5. which is looking for solutions.

This consciousness, in the case of water, must keep our attention focused on a preliminary priority list "before" solutions are arrived at.

Embarking on the solution to the water problem is only a job. Psyching people into the seriousness of the possible dilemma must occur somewhere early on the list of priorities, otherwise they may not assume responsibility and may not adapt seriously to the potential of the ongoing problem. It's somewhat akin to preparing a candidate for a political office where the necessary platform data for concurring is verbally stressed in general for specific causes "prior" to taking office. Then, the actual work unfold's, hopefully, in a combining effort and manner.

Suffice to say, understanding the nature of the impending chaos is forming in these mentioned priorities. Soon we will understand how the "project relief" fits into the massive puzzle that may form with community efforts in combating the inevitable "bake out" of humanity.

Emphasis must be large, dominantly inspired and meaningful to expect grand results "in" these priorities. The emphasis themselves on priorities must take precedence in order to inspire serious and definite action to begin and finish the project needed.

The actual project to offset the problem will only be as good as the combined efforts in displaying preventive measures. The measures are just around the corner in this book.

One of the first needs for accomplishing any community project is getting the attention of the people and politicians. Getting that attention for any reason is a project in itself. In this case, loosely assorted ideas of realistic facts intellectually or plainly described will suffice when sent or said to federal and state government representatives, philosophical societies, foundations for the preservation of this or that, science academies, library associations, international planners, newspapers, other hustling media plus neighbors, friends and relatives etc., etc.

Getting the attention needed for offsetting world chaos along with cooperating support from the public where the impending danger is circulating throughout will determine the right time for gathering the ideas from everyone concerned. This time is here now!

The suggestions arrived at as being the best will be accepted with the knowledge the project procedure is just as important, if not more, than the threat.

The main consensus is the initiators must strongly set the project in motion and continue through just as the greatest water dams were built and supplied enough power for the needs of society at the time.

Sure, the world's people understand we have problems blowing out of proportion and need rectifying attention as soon as possible.

Rectifying any situation requires two fold necessities. One is a realistically workable idea that can be proven to get the required results. The other one is, of course, money to promote the program. The program, in this case, is one of which everyone must face who wants to survive and cares about our future as living beings.

The buck must stop being passed to someone else. It's time for "everyone" to accept responsibilities of somekind appropriate to their ability. It's time for the people of the world to care a little or more about the function of our world wide survival and raise their standards in some manner as compared to just existing! It's time to stop well wishing and participate in some way. It's time for the world's people to work and think more about prevention methods instead of wearing masks to cover up their blemishes of fear, instability, low esteem, fantasies, inabilities and backwardness because of being abused at a young age or other inflicting abnormalities.

We've all had problems. Let's rise above them with unending belief where we "can" do it! Let's learn more how to cooperate as compared to opposing and fighting. Fighting only proves one thing. It only proves who is the best fighter. Only to be the best fighter is to say, "I have the biggest ego problem."

Is supporting an individual's or a nation's ego problem more important than for the survival of mankind on planet Earth?

Let's set the luxuries of life aside for awhile and concentrate and participate, in our own way, on the goal of preventing mankind's misery of deterioration just to become extinct because of ignorance, greed, egocentricity, indolence, bad attitude and other idiosyncrasies.

Let's, as they say in circles of meaningful causes, congregate in world efforts to centralize our goals of reducing these life pinching threats to a point where we can all be proud of that accomplishment together for a change.

Getting the attention of governments and politicians for enormous projects as legislating laws for controlling people to make totally necessary changes for survival as soon as possible may take effect too late! The damage will then consume us all and divinity or not, when it's too hot, it's too hot!

The only solution to the problem of heat and no water is for the people of the world to legally make strategic changes. Lobbying and mass rallies gets action. Then cooperation will help reverse the tide of disaster because everyone will understand it's totally necessary for all of us.

Chapter 4

Stretching the imagination for methods of solving the problem

Now we have arrived at, theoretically, arousing the preoccupied and sleeping public of the world so they may join, somehow, in their efforts to prevent the chaos of heat dilation leading to collapsed blood vessels to say the least. Any creeping misery can occur when one gets too hot in the environment.

It's time to unveil at least one plan by your author of which, hopefully, may influence or entice others to utilize their innovative or inventive abilities for the purpose of furthering the cause of helping to maintain mankind's constant existence on this planet as compared to melting, suffocating and/or burning up because they didn't care enough to do something about it!

The problem: Ozone disfiguration or insufficient balance is causing climate change. Attempts at correcting the situation are in process, but are moving like a snail. Government, bug business producers and overpopulation is resisting efforts to change.

Also, nature certainly does have a cyclical influence, but mankind's lust for progress is aggravating the natural course and is accelerating near future chaos through irresponsibility, carelessness and industrial overconsumption and development.

The excuse and cop-out now for not accepting responsibility to take action is where it takes too much time, effort, resources and money to reverse the existing ozone trend.

Around the world, technological advancements and war etc. are adding to the heat that burns the calories of oxygen and hydrogen with little relief in sight and is contributing toward robbing the environment of its remaining and normal temperature.

Next, there is still the ongoing problem of what to do about the nuclear waste they pack away into the ground and mountains.

All these mentioned conditions are disintegrating our atmospheric elements needed for life to exist on this earth.

Immediate and natural atmospherical miracles to offset these problems are completely unrealistic and only the deceived will expect them to occur. It is up to us to do our portion of the rectifying along with pending emissions control and industrial cooperation of many natures.

What kind of rectifier do we have available? It certainly isn't the water the fireman bring in for fires. That will help, but will only last a short time in view they are exhausting the sources.

How about turning down all the smokestacks in the world? That may help some along with other scientific methods which, it appears, has to be forced into place by highly and qualified influential people along with support of the general population. All this is certainly needed to help, but let's face it, time is running out and they are not seriously placing it as a priority.

We need "raw" material to cool the oncoming forces we face unless mankind is willing to accept the responsibility of becoming more conservative and really cut back on everything. Probably, the pressure taxing penalties of that approach will prevent industry growth and exist as somewhat, if not more, unrealistic.

If someone would invent a manner to exploit and expand hydrogen into mass water, that may be great, but is also unrealistic now and may not be congruent with nature.

Bringing many minds really together instead of congregating to oppose as do certain political so called reformers or initiators, has a good chance of forming substantial ideas that may bring an end to this dilemma.

However, in the meantime, there is only one resource available at present that can be an effective source of resolution when it is dealing with dampening, wetting or stamping out fire, heat and heat creators. Generally speaking, it "is" water.

If we are unable to filter or reserve enough water to cool our hot problems instigated by technological advancements and stop overpopulation etc., then we may have to resort to the only resource left at our disposal for at least some, if not more, of our hot industries and incidences; sea water. It won't be for drinking purposes, but it will surely conserve our fresh water until such a time when we have overcome our fears of extinction through future innovations and some very needed help from nature which may not be so realistic either.

What to do with the nuclear waste problem will be addressed in an appropriate space ahead.

Yes, sea water. Sound crazy? Others have already thought of it? That's possible. Your author doesn't claim to know everything everyone else ever thought of.

The scheme offered here works in model form as compared to what can exist in reality. Many famous buildings of the world, if not all, formed as a result of months and/or years of architectural design work "and" mechanical models of the projects. They have almost always proven to be workable and practical.

This project can prove its workability and practicability too and it won't unveil unprecedented costs especially when it is compared to the cost of human and animal etc. deterioration and extinction.

There is plenty of sea water to share around the globe which doesn't necessarily have to be utilized for all household use. There will be plenty of fresh water available for consumption purposes as household, restaurant and business buildings etc. when sea water takes the place of water used for farming, fires, commercial and industrial purposes, some household, pools, combating mob violence, industrial cooling, industrial filters, dirt roads, water spectaculars, man-made lakes, street cleaning and many other imaginable uses.

This project will move overflowing sea water into higher ground and sink into the ground wherever needed thereby helping to cool the earth.

Surely we like to nourish the thought where mankind's technological, while humble, abilities will sooner than later solve, resolve and "cure" the overburdening problem of climate change that we created with more advanced innovation than is currently available, but that is apparently in the future; not now. A little more of this in chapter five.

Remember, the whole world, according to some schools of thought and research, was covered with some kind of water at one time and the possibility of it being salty then as well as now is great. We can deal with salt a lot easier than extinction.

This offer of possibilities is contentious where sea water can be brought in across the nations from the shores of continents not by truckloads, plane loads or train loads, but by the methodical process of piping.

Needless to say, piping water, gas, oil and other necessary liquids for the higher standards of progress has proven sufficient and successful enough to be accepted and continue through into its distant future; why not sea water to assist the cause of survival into the foreseeable future?

The system of piping is, again, a practical and workable program of which will contribute toward eliminating inefficiency of fire fighting especially in the forest/brush areas rendering insufficient water. This method will allow access to many more hydrants throughout the globe and especially vulnerable areas by method of manual water access plus automatic spraying systems. When the time is right, there will be a way of designing this system in a practical and efficient manner.

The costs for installation won't be as much as maybe preliminarily estimated because this system won't be in constant volume use as a commercial air conditioning system or household plumbing. Preliminary and tentative design of the system will unfold beginning in the next chapter.

The salt in sea water will help put out the fires quicker and the minerals will help fertilize the ground. It is totally necessary for us to evaluate all the advantages of sea water and the practicability of it in contrast to the disadvantages and arrive at the best route to travel in pursuit of preventing chaos so the disadvantages do not outweigh the advantages. It is important for more minds than less to do that evaluation because, needless to say, this will be a tremendously vast encounter by friendly and/ or not so friendly people of the world attempting to join with their different accessibilities, sources and resources. That includes material, mechanical, physical, cultural, social, mental and emotional resources among others such as very loving and cooperative plus exasperating, dissonant and resistant attitudes; all of which are needed for this once in history world community affair.

Half the battle to succeed in the following project guidelines is not only the preparation of design and application, but the preparation of different kinds of people convincing each other how to work together in a common challenge. This deserves as much attention as the project itself. That is part of the reason why these scripts may appear a little repetitious in expression. Hopefully, the readers will do something similar when relating to others concerning this needed effort. Specific repetition in this study can be helpful in the promotion of these efforts.

Mankind has had lots of challenges and opponents in their history on Earth, but never an opponent of this immense and almost mystifying nature where all mankind is in a position of having to change their ways in a major manner for the sake of all mankind's survival.

Since we don't really see much of any super great threat evidence of oncoming disaster unfolding at present, it's easy to sit back and do nothing. That's a super great indication we "won't" survive at that rate.

Chapter 5

Initial ideas and innovation for solving the problem

The sea and other waters will always remain in equilibrium. That is, no continent will suffer noticeable declination in their shoreline in relationship to any other continent.

Planet Earth does not exist as a smoothly rounded sphere. It has a jagged surface of mountains several miles high in many places and for the benefit of this proposed project, ocean depths are several miles deep in other areas.

Water used for purposes mentioned in chapter four is hardly measurable when it is compared to the almost immeasurable amount of water in the oceans of the world.

Chances are more favorable than less or not, when utilized as a supplement for the survival problem, sea water declination will probably not be significantly or feasibly noticed for possibly many centuries. By that time, mankind will have advanced through eras of change meaningful enough to have solved for problems of even greater challenges and approach the problem of climate change in a manner of which we are presently unaware. If they don't, it won't matter anyway. If they moved progressively into an opposite destiny of doom or even of continued deteriorating, it will probably be an indication a dying earth of living beings is inevitable. Dealing with that possibility, as any other major calamity, is only part of the "whole" universe function and a little unrealistic for us to be burdened with considering, solving or changing.

Utilizing sea water, at present, appears to be a reasonable method of supplementation for our oncoming water and temperature confrontation.

Water declination, along with a rise in ambient world wide temperature, can be combated with an evenly spread sea water system that can be regulated world wide so hot areas can be cooled to a more desirable degree.

Hot areas are mainly where there are fires, deserts and ineffectively regulated industrial output.

Secondarily, sea water can replace many water needed programs and necessities as mentioned in chapter four to say nothing of the need to water new forest plants. Where rain is plenty, there are trees. Trees are vitally needed and must be replanted and watered after fires. They won't amply grow without water; any kind of water.

Third and not necessarily last, sea water access will serve as a multiple source of moisture and coolant for large areas of residential grass and plants, business parks and golf course purposes. Its all primarily for the preservation and maintenance of continued even temperature for all living beings.

The science of sea water distribution will require a brand new education for all and must be adhered to by all for what may be termed as a much needed survival consciousness which is just as meaningfully needed as any other spiritually oriented consciousness.

Water consciousness must exist along with its partner sea water distribution. A proposed distribution system will begin with an agreement comprised of world leaders supported by their people to tap into the ocean at specifically arrived at intervals along continental coastlines or there about.

The places appropriated for tapping into the water will be sites for concrete enclosed pumps on the beach controlled by automatic and serviceable solar energy or the waves.

The pumps and pipes will be located at planned intervals and directions according to strategic land availability and need.

Each pump unit will begin with an engineered size return water filter section pulling water through it and into the pump which will be located somewhere upstream on dry land.

The pump unit will set on a stand which is fastened to the ground and the supply pipe is pointed in an inland direction. That supply pipe will be a material of galvanized or heavy duty plastic or fibrous pipe which, if available, will connect with a satellite remotely controlled damper for necessary regulating near the pump (optional).

These pumps, depending on where they are specifically located, will or can be erected on the ground, on brackets, through mountain drilled holes suspended or supported at any approved height. Manuel and/or remote dampers are recommended for velocity or damage control where needed.

Periodical snakeout access is recommended to prevent or cleanout chemical buildup or gathered debree which may be a result of a plugged or broken water filter.

Attaching pipes firmly will prevent rattling, vibrating or other movements of which may be mechanically detrimental to longterm quality and efficiency.

An option to use noncorrosive plastic or fibrous type pipe may be utilized if approved by local planners. A warning is issued now to use caution considering a joining of two materials of which may render incompatible and create a chemical deterioration such as electrolyses or similar reactions.

The piping project has the same general possibilities for installing as any plumbing or electrical installation. That is, the pipes may be subjected to extending in a forty five or ninety degree angle or curve where totally necessary with the engineering awareness of the more turns there are, the more resistance there is to constant volume and velocity. Straight line flow for longer run distances carry's increased advantages.

Periodical pump boosters will be needed to sustain pressure. Boosters will include pressure evaluation of intake and supply water. If pressure isn't sufficient at any point when triggered for use, the closest pump will activate; thereby the prior pump will receive the lack of pressure message and activate sending the same message to its prior pump, if needed. Remember, these pipes won't all be running constantly, so constant pressure isn't needed. Instant flow from constant pressure on one pipe may be an invalid expectation. A little patience will pay.

Distribution areas with automatic sprinklers for fires may have exceptions in constant velocity for quicker flow.

Note: Fires, especially forest or brush fire may be running neck and neck with contributing factors toward climate change. Not only are the fires themselves very hot, but the gaseous effects from them, the bald places left for exposure to the elements and the lack of rain because of no precipitation magnetism, creates area warming. A continuous basis of this kind of treatment globally adds toward the inevitable increase in temperature which, in turn, manifests more of the same if not checked. Fire departments will welcome this project.

By the time this project is ready to commence, either sufficient or not so sufficient financing may be available. Hence, the usual changes of the times may influence availability, quality and various directions in procedure. This is mentioned now so the actual preparation will only follow suit of people who are actually doing the initiating. All may not unfold as is proposed here without cooperative and chronological procedure.

The sea water will reach its destination from either straight flow (minimum turns) or a more complex system of branch lines and extensions off the main, second or third pipes.

Branch pipes may run on a slight curve akin to railroad tracks and will consist of three to four inch pipe unless engineering requires stringent and provable differences.

International project innovators must agree on an estimated use of sea water and the even distribution over the globe. Smaller islands with minor contributing factors will be exempt to this program.

A calculation, determined by a global committee for joint efforts, will arrive at the amount of cubic feet per minute of sea water utilized for areas most effected by climate change and areas where population expansion has the appearance of contributing more to the warming. Those continents with higher intensity will not totally fall into the category of highest contributors toward the climate change. Example: Highest contributors may be a nation letting a fire burn until its out as compared to one that has a priority on extinguishing it readily (just an example; not a rule).

The global committee will also be responsible for determining an ongoing effect of the system which won't amount to much more than simple calculations of periodical temperature and humidity etc. First will be to gain a global perspective and second will be local vicinity readings. Also, the committee will be responsible for relaying instructions for regulating in specific areas chosen. Specific areas globally will, of course, employ representatives to manage the proper mechanical regulations, adjustments and repairs.

All installed materials will be owned and operated by each nation's government unless the committee disagrees. The advantage is where it will allow many new jobs distributed throughout the nations for the installation and maintenance of the system. Government control "may" be more effective, consistent and reliable. That, of course, is always open for probing, discussion or debate among those who display genuine interest in achieving best action and results.

Chapter 6

The many meetings for approval; discouraging or helpful

Committee meetings are generally comprised for the purpose of making decisions, right? Well, the committee mentioned in chapter five may have to accept more responsibility than just thinking and talking.

If the committee delegates too many decisions out for processing by other agencies, the system project may become too complicated and expensive thereby stagnating the progress.

We don't only want the benefits of this project for our inheritors, but also for the present living generations who are initiating the project. Let's keep it simple as possible.

It would behoove the process of progress in this project for the committee members to at least travel from place to place displaying some form of directing and guiding the local contractors etc. similar to that which the United Nations do so excessive time is not wasted.

Let the committee accept more responsibility for details and have them maintain their own agenda and keep track of their activity. Any disruption in progress can be easily detected by others who are involved. The committee must be sufficiently backed and bonded for project efficiency and scheduling etc. so there is no hierarchy, illegal manipulation tendencies that may be irresistible in acquiring.

Every step on the sea water road map of progress must be clearly exposed to the public world wide so the project is not only wholly and enthusiastically accepted, but also supported. That means each nation will spread the word to its own people. This is mentioned because efforts to build a system of prevention doesn't particularly have an appearance of flair, glory or community excitement for any one person or group. There isn't much to see and what there is; is just work. People don't always recognize the fruit of effort; even when their health or lives are spared over a period of time, so they need reminding.

The system and its progress must be made to stand out as an accomplishment of being proud of how we are all somehow making our contribution toward quenching the inevitable climate change threat.

Whosoever forms the committee, plus the committee members themselves, may hesitate in their efforts. They must be reminded the inevitable ice age will eventually cool things off, but do we want to wait for that very slowly emerging event? It may run into millenniums before there is a noticeable change. Besides, if we can stay alive long enough to gain enough technical or wise brainstorms, we may be able to offset some of these natural and man-made inevitabilities a little more permanently for the future of mankind.

Bringing nations together in mutual projects favorable to all will help stabilize the emerging tendencies to conquer and dominate one another by process of subjugation, enslavery, manipulation, gross competition, exploitation or wars.

Advantages of the sea water project and system:

1. Sea water is plentiful.
2. Sea water blends into the ground anywhere because it is made up of H2O and minerals.
3. Sea water "can" be transferred.
4. The salt will tend to clean the pipes and snuff out the fires.
5. The project will be a boon to the employment situation globally.
6. The project will foster global unity at least to some extent.

7. The filtering will tend to clean the sea water locally especially if the filtering system is designed for larger capacity which will be more of a sophisticated undertaking.

8. More water will be available for most areas where water conservation cannot be seriously considered such as mountain forests, commercial sites, residential fires and wherever other conditions require high velocity hose water for fires and/or explosions.

9. There will be more advantages as discoveries unfold.

Properly distributed sea water will help equalize climate temperatures.

Deserts and areas without trees and brush may not be subjected to this system. This saves project money. The exception to that is where and when the community of the world agrees on exploiting and developing baron lands for population settling depending, of course, on sea water allowance.

The project of the sea water distribution system must be viewed perspectively and conservatively for arriving at best results, not emotionally or in a state of panic just because we are worried or because we may want to create jobs etc.

Spiritually, there are those who believe God will direct the course and those are profoundly supported beliefs of which are to be respected, observed, considered and dealt with in a communal type manner; not in a manner of which is oppositionally manipulative because of inflexible mannerisms of belief. Rationality, objectivity and belief, however it applics, will guide and lead the direction of this particular road map resolution. Another view that seems to be a little more universally accepted is that famous adage or proverb, spiritually or not so spiritually, "God helps those who help themselves." All the spiritually and nonspiritually oriented contributors of the project initiation, discussion, legislation, action committee, organizing or other promotions and even some constructional opposition will be largely helpful in maintaining a peace in nonpartisan mannerisms by seriously and broadly recognizing the flexible value and advantages of that quoted phrase.

When the initiators of the sea water project gain a beachhead of progress based on omen, fear, belief or scientific evaluation, the key to the project success will exist in the ability to be persistent in maintaining a solid, but flexible "belief" where this project is the best route to stimulate and embark upon with objectivity to solve and resolve this ongoing threat toward the existence of all living beings.

This world threatening phenomenon approaches in a two fold manner; partly by nature and partly by mankind. Nature might be a very difficult task to alter, but the devastation mankind creates "is" alterable. We "can" manage that alteration if we choose to do it. Let's choose it.

The whole picture option in perspective can be accomplished from beginning to end by utilizing the grandest tools available; insight, creativity, determination, patience, understanding and tolerance just as any other achievable endeavor.

There is no denying this will be a number one global effort. The first of its kind where all of mankind, with a very few exceptions, will pool their efforts toward one mutual cause. A few nations are dabbling at reducing climate change, but they are dragging along with insufficient momentum almost as with an attitude of, "Oh well, we won't be here when it gets rough." That tends to defeat our objectives.

Avoidance of reality is unprecedented and unphilosophical. That is an immense factor that adds to the bulk of ignorant, narrow and self-centered attitudes.

A dialogue supporting the project may include "We are at a time, in this space of life which may be only on planet Earth that we know of, whereby there is an opportunity to unite in a global project of which may result in mankind really caring about one another as compared to the hardline self or group centered mentality who are obliviously and/or unmindful to and with others.

We, the people of the world, have a chance to expose ourselves to unity more than ever. Maybe this will be the opportunity we have been hoping for; global cooperation as compared to global competition where dominance seems primary.

Any communal or community project will only move forward when there is a need or when an initiator is convincing enough in influencing others to join and form a momentum to propel it into motion. That's what this chapter in particular is about.

That which is important many times flys right by the observer without recognition or consideration.

Maybe it's because the other person or persons didn't think of it first (ego) or because they were preoccupied with something that seemed more important such as what's in it for them.

This system of sea water supplementation must have a plan behind it that will "grab" people's attention. The project initiators must create a plan that will inspire, frighten, enlighten, entice, worry or somehow influence individuals, groups or masses in paying attention to what is offered in a similar manner to that of any great crusade or event.

World dichotomy must be prevented by stressing efforts of joining possibly to the point of exacerbating in necessity efforts to offset climate change in "any" manner.

Increased advertising on climate change cause/ effect is essential for the promotion of this project. The people as well as the initiators must be convinced so the project will be supported by all. TV sponsors will be needed for disseminating the cause/effect and relief. All institutions where people gather (ch.3) must be notified and educated for this inevitability. Government officials and private organizations must work together not anymore as coalitions opposing other factions, but as partners in one cause; for preserving our world temperatures and air.

Committees must be formed for this project, but they must also be overseen by others similar to the checks and balance system. Mutual trust has been somewhat nebulous in forming societies and community projects in general, so a little more watching each other won't hurt and with really needed projects as this, maybe that need for watching can be reduced in time with enough insight, belief and trust consciousness. It "can" spread and become a factor leading toward more compatibility among all.

We, the people of the world, are capable of and can cooperate and support a cause for a more compatible society of human beings or we can and will constantly oppose one another which, of course, will end in conflicts, wars, dismay and no end of self-defeating species as compared to our animal counterparts in nature. Let's decide what we will do.

Most animal life eat each other when they can, alive or dead, for purposes of survival and have been doing it for millions of years without ado and they have still survived; until now with our selfishness. They lived with nature. We haven't.

Mankind, with all our supposedly virtuous respect for each other's carcasses are philosophical concerning our existence in a delusive manner. We haven't been serious "about" our existence. We "must" change that with more creative and caring meetings.

Chapter 7

Secondary planning and approval for project procedure

First in the process of planning is organizing for cooling the effects, generally. That's all about rearranging what we have here on planet Earth.

Second in the process of planning is to offset our environmental deterioration from population expansion and nuclear waste contamination. The expansion is great for capital growth, but the contamination is a following side effect. That will add to our deterioration.

How do we rid ourselves of waste; especially the nuclear type? Burying it under mountains seems to be the only method at present. As time unfolds, that can present disastrous problems!

Household waste is dug into and becomes part of the ground where it decays with other decaying earth if graded and packed properly. However, nuclear waste is canned in material of which is vulnerable in time and may seep through our mineral and/or moisture makeup and not only contribute toward living being's toxically influenced deterioration, but when it escapes into specific substances, can cause a transformation into heat form with unheard of consequences adding to more climate change. Remember, this is mostly due to the progress of population expansion. We must learn more how to deal with and offset these conditions.

Move the stuff out of Earth's pull of gravity and keep it going by a system of small train like rocketeering. Comparatively small rockets can propel many lightweight barrels of waste into space. Those barrels can be designed to deteriorate in time and become a natural phenomenon of the universe. The rocket engines and/or boosters can be retrieved, as experience has shown and be used many times. The words train like means link the barrels together similar to prisoners and pull them into space. There is plenty of space in the universe and the barrels would appear as a half of a drop in the bucket out there. Eventually, they will disperse into space unnoticed.

Another possibility would be to build a giant jet like gun and "shoot" large bullets filled with, primarily, nuclear waste. That waste is about the only substance mankind has no use for yet. Let's discharge it from our planet and peaceably use nuclear power for our needs without anxiety concerning the contamination of waste material.

Secondary planning will unveil many new possibilities of cooling the globe on the surface because more research will evoke new methods and products needed when innovators understand a greater need than ever is at hand. Now is the time to promote the joint efforts and peaceful plans of attack that will be surprisingly helpful as a source of progress momentum in conquering a threatening monster.

There will be meetings galore around the world and these meetings will be aimed at attacking one major objective; reducing and maybe even conquering climate change with its added hazards of nuclear waste.

The best thing mankind has ever and will ever have is not love or money, but the ability to effectively communicate with others. During times of potential disaster, love or money is second, third or whatever down the line. All the energies extended wouldn't exist without communication of procedure. That's what is primarily needed for the promotion of this project.

Everyone must purposely gain increased consciousness of more communicable mannerism so world cooperation will commence and proceed in community halls, churches, government meetings, schools, businesses, at work, offices, residential neighborhoods, dances, bars, hangouts, backyards and so many places where people are talking or listening. Maybe it's time they start talking about something "really" important; like preserving life.

It's time for all to join, some way, in this project to save our earth's surface for survival especially, beside surviving, so we can set an inspiring example for future generations to recognize and possibly follow.

Chapter 8

Acquiring support of the people

Acquiring support of the people is usually a matter of contacting people nationally or locally. This case of world cooperation requires a task of a little different nature in view of it being a world wide effort.

Getting started acquiring that support, as always, is sometimes more difficult than estimated. First things must rain as first or general chaos may linger as mentioned. We must not allow that to happen.

The very first step is to get people inspired for listening. Your author is doing just that here and now. When the word gets around, others will acquire their own inspiration and spread the word in their own manner.

This project "will" unfold and progress "will" increase as the word travels. Soon after, the necessity and proposed project will have the attention of political and private legislative and developmental promoters. When those steps have commenced, the people are encouraged to call political representatives from their local areas and express their views. Following the attention grabbing and gossip stage of the progress, the word of immediate necessity will begin to form. That's where continuous interest, support in many ways and cooperation becomes the greatest asset to the program.

This impending danger/disaster will affect everyone everywhere, so it is necessary for everyone to become a part of the project movement. Volunteers for survival will form and inspire people to participate for living into the future and work toward our common goal of maintaining life on this planet instead of being indifferent and incinerating away.

The balance of the stages, after the first, will be a series of branch line planning and adjustments along with learning and practicing world cooperation among the people. If humanity on Earth would adapt from a philosophy of stating "the" people of Earth or "them" to one stating "our" people of Earth or "us," we would, indeed, become closer with meaningful cooperation in this endeavor to survive. That's the consciousness that builds family, not families. World family is what we need now. Families are very spread out individual entities and only good for their own cause. This cause is for "all" of us.

This project will work better as a world family and "can" inspire mankind to cooperate with one another in world mutuality as compared to world domination or world avoidance; especially in a critical time of surviving needs. We may not have another chance, so let's not gamble with the lives of our species and all other living beings of which have inherited the Earth.

Where any large project comes successfully together, money of some kind has been traditionally the backbone of barter. Presently, it appears it always will. As the population has grown and mankind has slipped into a quandary of mastering, gaining, controlling and much of the time greedily having and keeping everything possible, we have also relinquished value learned from the "golden rule." Let's reinstate it as a guideline for our progress.

The cooperation with one another derived from the value of the golden rule can and/or will be at least equal to the value of the dictatorial medium where money instigates or rules. What this means is, in the context of promoting and hastening results of this project, cooperation is needed to move forward in saving time, money and lives instead of haggling and fighting over who is boss or who's money to use etc., etc. Every time they argue and fight over who is right because of political basics (party line belief), mass ego mania sets in causing undue resistance and progress barriers. When that happens, money, many times is squandered where arguments do nothing except prove who is the most successful at arguing;

nothing else. That capital lost could have been utilized for more important issues such as the project to survive. They must be reminded— time and money "can" be a matter of "staying alive" on planet Earth.

Any exposure to benefits allowing savings on unneeded costs will mean we as people, not as lord ruler masters, dictators or partisan administrators will at least reduce, if not eliminate, a political and private dichotomy that prevents meaningful action and progress. This must be high on an agenda of priorities for this program.

The project to save all living beings from a torturous end may be as difficult to expedite as any other political initiative, but where there is a will to survive, there will be a will to convince. We are "all" in the same boat similar to the much smaller scaled dilemma in the supposed days of Noah's Arc. At least their temperature and air was probably good. What a far cry from the drying up world of today. Let's fix it. We have to. We "can." Let's develop the spirit to win.

Years and centuries ago we had little methods of communicating from one nation to another in a short period of time for emergency or strategic purposes and only created small and local problems with much less people.

Now we can talk to anyone around the world immediately and have a much larger necessity of communicating with more and extensive problems with more people.

Our expansion and technological growth has brought us necessities and luxuries, plus bigger problems than ever; one of which is the threat of unbearable heat and diminishing fresh water. Now it's our capable duty to efficiently handle reducing that real threat through masterminding a scheme for offsetting it. Let's get with it! It's up to all of us.

Yes, these words of alert warning are repeated over and over and must follow suit around the world for our survival.

Chapter 9

Visualizing results in perspective and reality

Most all humans seem to agree we want to live, generally. That's what this book is also about.

There are spiritual views, of course, indicating life on Earth is only a stepping stone toward their destiny and not to be so seriously concerned about preserving it or even the planet. Sometimes pain and suffering to the end changes or alters that belief or perception, if you will.

The project for relief, in this book, is for "everyone" regardless of their views on existence or destiny.

Reality is conceived and perceived based on belief whether it be inherited, exploit oriented or chosen without influence.

The belief where suffering to the end is predestined is profound and seems unbendable to many in these spiritual views. It may be, if the greater majority exists profoundly with predestined philosophy, where the balance of people on Earth will have to assume the responsibility for the project. Questioning what the mass of mankind may or may not do has little value because belief and survival is always subject to the whims and birthright choices of everyone.

Regardless of general philosophy or spirituality, we all have a birthright to choose or change anything in particular and especially if it means contributing toward any form of coexistence and/or pleasure. It certainly is a pleasure to feel normally cool and alive! Maybe that's enough to alter a belief a bit, like they say just in case, as mentioned, of being mistaken. Of course, that works both ways. Flexibility is always available for all.

When the project for sea water distribution is in full motion due to the suggested world cooperation instead of world conflict, everyone will experience a time of peace in particular because life deterioration will no longer be imminent due to bad habits mankind had adopted such as living by the rules of dominancy, deception, self-centeredness and greed.

The results of cooperation in combating climate change and waste hazards will render a proud, honorable and much more compatible society of mankind.

Mankind will have assumed and taken responsibility for offsetting the destiny they have created. This is only part of the whole scene.

The appreciation gained because of all these wonderful changes will, like a "good" disease, infect business organizations to follow suit reducing "smokestack" infestation. Cooperative attitudes are infectious too.

The results of the project will relieve the earth's surface of fires from natural and man-made sources much quicker without fresh water as mentioned earlier and will serve as replacement water for a host of industrial, decorative and agricultural needs to say nothing of man-made lakes, golf courses, parks and other projects requiring water.

The cooperation of cooling hot areas with sea water will offset climate change until industry and technology follows with new innovations. It will happen! Mankind just needs incentive to follow through in their adjustments for change. The project offers exposure to incentive. Once mankind has adopted that incentive, they will follow their paths of design and move forward.

Dealing with reality is relatively conjunctive with spiritual belief. When the world's people decide this project is accepting responsibility to make changes, the belief however it is consecrated, goes to work just as do the promoters, employees, volunteers and other help. Efforts of all will arrange their beliefs for the common cause. That is spirituality and reality blending for success! The goals are the same. There is no reason to separate people because of the manner in which they believe.

Without brains, bodies and hands, nothing gets accomplished. Belief is a supporter. Let it do "its" work. Believe in this method of offsetting disaster or do not believe in it. Just don't stand on the fence.

The odds appear doing nothing, other than the insufficient progress at present, will result in the inevitable torturous death of all living beings. If there is any hell, temperatures beyond the usual may be an introduction. That, of course, is strictly hypothetical at this time, but deserves rational observation.

The odds appear the project of sea water will help retain endurable temperatures for a lengthily period and allow us fresh water to survive. This is a time of new opportunities for mankind's survival. Let's not shun it.

Sure, the beaches will change somewhat. Most beaches of the world taper downward; some slowly and others a little quicker. The waterline will elevate from the shore inward. Shores with little or no sandy beaches or where there are cliffs and the water is precipitously deep, the elevation will be more noticed.

Will it all resolve naturally in time without doing anything? Yes, because everything resolves with the long term passage of time. No, because the lives of us and our next generations won't last that long with climate change the way it is progressing now.

The earth has given us everything we have needed for quite a length of time without demanding a return. Now it's time to give back especially since we have only received.

The beaches won't be normal in the short term ahead. Those ice caps and snowy mountains are melting and beginning to raise the ocean's levels. The threat of coastline property, especially, will be under water until climate change dries up everything to a frazzle including all living beings; that is, with mankind's continuous displacement of the ozone factor through the smoke of industry and motor vehicles. This is estimated to happen in the lifetime of many of us of who are here today to say nothing, again, of our descendants.

Now, does the project sound a little better? Governments of the world aren't motivated enough to take initial action with climate change solutions without support of the people. It's up to all of us to let them know we want action now!

Doing nothing isn't intelligent or safe. Why? When living beings are all gone as a result of doing nothing, the greater majority of climate change and the nuclear waste problem will no longer exist. Sad, there won't be anyone to strive, care or worry anymore ever and the design of Earth will resume its equilibrium; maybe. It may also become too late for that.

Indeed it "is" negative thinking to do nothing. Positive thinking is to do something about it all. If a vote is required, vote it in and enjoy and be proud, contented and happy for the great accomplishment mankind has the ability to encounter and complete.

Getting involved in this ever so needed worldwide effort is not only needed for all living beings, it will also make a much overdue and better world of humans who will exercise their pride of being earthly humans for maintaining this world of which we have been born into for a priceless period of time and leave planet Earth in better shape than entering into it. Wishful thinking? That's what they said about Rome.

Chapter 10

Catalyst for success

Ever since man began the urge to populate, they had setbacks and dilemmas galore. Those were integral segments of their progress in moving forward. So far, they have succeeded in that process regardless of the endless problems and as of yet, haven't subsided or surrendered to the obvious forces of resistance and influence. Finally, we are faced with those possibilities of becoming extinct along with the balance of all other surface living beings. We are now faced with having to decide what our destiny will be. That destiny will unfold according to the decisions of effort extended "by" the people who volunteer those efforts. Without them, we are probable goners.

The unmentionable of planet Earth becoming a dead planet and uninhabitable for the most part won't happen; at least not in the foreseeable future. Only surface living beings will perish. Subsurface and small creatures living without light and little air will probably survive particularly because when mankind has perished, the problems of climate change and waste contamination will subside, as mentioned in chapter nine and disappear thereby allowing the recycling of living beings in, of course, very small proportion and size; certainly not like us. It's been said that may be the manner in which all living beings began. Life conception theories vary so distinctively which adds to community isolation and social dismay.

Negative scenarios must be expressed in every situation where decisions are needed so resolutions may unfold when it pertains to reference of believing ("I believe this project will work." "I don't believe in tinkering with man's destiny.").

Regardless of whether they were justified as being right and proper or not, wars would never have been won, beliefs would never have been secured and buildings would never have been built without the medium exercise of communicating and cooperation. Mankind is still attempting to do it, but the quality, insight and genuine caring of that communicating is lacking and sliding at times when compared to the rate of technological progress of present time. That's what needs balancing for meaningful projects to begin and conclude successfully. We "can" do it.

Communicating and cooperating is not only a dire necessity, but also an art. As in any art, it needs to be constantly improved, expounded upon, developed and polished for best appearance and value.

The proposed project must be treated in a similar manner. The dilemma first needs clarifying as to what it is, what it can be and what position it will move into. Then, the objective of displaying an exact replica of how the whole picture can and/or will unfold will be realized for proceeding. We are close to that point.

Inevitably, the better picture will transform, indeed, through necessity and determined desire of communicating and cooperating. That's an art of caring and will increase the value in that venture of enthusiasm which can set off a chain reaction for desire of human survival.

That's one of the catalysts until someone has discovered a better or added manner which will allow the project to unfold successfully and continue into the future with controlled regulation of expansion and population.

While viewing the problem of climate change, waste disposal and deciding which route to engage, consider the following for determining whether or not this situation is serious enough to pursue as a participator in some manner for the benefit of "offsetting" the coming dilemma of which we have all created for a long time.

The surface of the globe is the only area where there is earthquake activity. Those land shifts may be fairly deep into the ground, but relatively speaking, they are still closer to the surface than the intrinsic depths of Earth. Someday we may venture into treating the earth, but presently our concern is to control ourselves on the surface.

Anything on the surface of anything is always more vulnerable. Earthquakes are cracks as in a mud pie. The hotter the mud, the more and deeper cracks occur. Earth is doing the same. It always has and from our puny perspective, always will be. Dealing with now though, we must consider how they fit in with climate change and its eccentric temperature variations.

Take note of how often these quakes occur as compared to how often they occurred fifty or a hundred years ago or more. If you observe they are occurring more rapidly, that is an accelerated pace that can be an indication of increased heat causing earth's plates and plain ordinary cracks to shrink as in the mud pie or better still; African, Australian, etc. and other dry plains of land. The cracks may not be clearly visible because of wind, dirt, sand and some vegetation overgrowth covering them, but they are there. More quakes are also a sign of climate change.

Staying interested while observing and researching earthquake acceleration can add toward factors which indicates the ambient temperature just under and above the surface is approaching at an increasing rate of rapidity. When an alarm rings, it pays to do something or pay the consequences. Under ocean quakes are part of it all.

History has shown earthquake cracks have gobbled up thousands of people. Now, with the present rate of climate change not being corrected or at least offset, these cracks will reach to the surface and be repeated performances; only on a much more accelerated scale.

Possibilities are such where nuclear waste barrels are buried, they will break just as a nut is cracked and spread the unwanted material throughout the surface and around the involved areas; possibly globally.

Sure, earthquakes have been known to be part of the globe's normal functioning. That's as close to natural as we can decipher. What we must be alarmed with is how often, how many and how evenly spread they occur.

If the climate change and waste problem isn't corrected quite soon, the surface of our world may, more than not, become a jiggling jagged hotplate only to slowly consume its living combatants for nutritionally nourishing the soil. After that, as mentioned twice before, everything will resume to its normal state. What a massive vitamin. Too bad we have to be cooked and consumed!

Temperatures on this globe are not balanced. Let's balance them through the proposed methods.

Nuclear power will be a way of life in the not so distant future. Whenever this type of power is produced, there is a certain amount of waste material that must be set aside. So far, a use for it hasn't been discovered. If the containers are of superior material, they will drain the earth of valuable and needed resources. If they are made of inferior material, the contents will eventually seep out and contaminate our earth below and above the surface.

We cannot allow the contaminating waste to sit until a need for it is discovered any more than a need for cadavers or human and animal excrement. The nuclear waste has to go! The only feasible and safe solution is as mentioned; send it out into space.

Remember, nuclear power is here to stay and those containers will multiply to an unbearable extent over long periods of time. Presently, there is no problem, but long term accumulation can present a leaking condition. Let's tackle that job now!

Sea water transferred inland releasing and draining into and through the ground will be filtered through the ground and become fresh water for utility purposes (this statement must be further evaluated and confirmed for its validity by global water distribution departments).

Another method to offset climate change while science and government are working on solutions and approach, is to extract material from the mountains or wherever for the purpose of transferring it to pumped out oil spaces, then fill the oil cavities which have been drained all those years. The material will serve as an insulator similar to that of the original oil so the surface of the earth will maintain a normal temperature. Sure, it will be an immense job as will be the piping project, but isn't it worth it for helping to save all living beings?

There are people who are skeptical of any climate change existence. They believe mankind isn't the cause of it all and do not believe it is a threat at present. Many claim the earth cycles periodically from hot to freezing and back to hot etc. over many millenniums where this period of time is just part of that cycle. The very dangerous part of that belief exists in the evidence where #1, the cycle of temperature has historically occurred slowly without sudden alarm. #2, climate change has only been noticed within the past hundred years or so ironically and parallel with the progressively accelerating oil drilling throughout the world. The more oil extracted, the more climate change is noticed.

New energy sources with less side effects must be discovered. The question is, will mankind survive long enough to develop and use them at the rate we are going by not being serious enough about offsetting climate change?

Mankind must become more alerted and aware to prepare for and against future calamity. Without it, again, all life will cease to exist. Acting now may prevent disaster. Acting later may be too late.

If, by some unforeseeable reason, the people, science, industry and governments of the world do not accept the sea water project, that's unfortunate for all of us unless they have a better and workable plan that will offset beginning momentum right away!

An alternative to reducing this inevitable scorcher is to methodically and progressively reduce the population by by means of not allowing large families. This will work along with other methods. It just means humanity will have to gain control over and regulate their emotions, ideals and spiritual beliefs in particular if they want humanity to survive. Sure, the side effect would be less growth. That's a small price to pay for keeping our species alive.

The significance of offsetting climate change by piping sea water inland will serve more beneficially as a replacement of fresh water in more places slowly evaporating because of the climate dilemma and will help to reduce the devastating effect of sea water rising onto the continents as a result of melting icebergs.

Let's call this sea water project a temporary supplement for survival while mankind is struggling to curb greenhouse affects causing climate change and its effects.

The worst that can happen if we don't have enough perseverance in convincing other people and governments to initiate strict change on industrial affects and oil products output including autos, planes, boats etc., etc. is a steady drying up of anything of which cannot live in heat way over our usual temperature; especially without fresh water. The best that can happen will result from world cooperation.

If the contents of this book makes sense to you the reader, spread the word to everyone, especially to global leaders to "get going." We don't have much time left. When it's too late, it's too late.

Research has shown, cylindrical cores of earth's samples, where very cold and very hot ages of time has lasted from centuries to millenniums without accurate and consistent indications of how long the time span would be although mankind "has" learned more about time lengths of the "ice ages" than of the "heat ages."

Most humans aren't too concerned about a time of everything turning to ice because of not being here when it happens. The "heat age" is very rapidly approaching us and that is verified by those cyndrical core samples and much more scientific data. They have recently claimed climate change is no longer a speculation. It has been working up to it for centuries and arriving faster now with the chemical changes mankind has instigated and promoted with their accelerating progress in all areas.

Assuming the heat age may be only a few degrees hotter so everyone has to have air conditioning is a reasonable manner of thought even though that entails a completely different manner of life style and believing. Relying on that possible heat limit may be a very erroneous deduction and complete shock to a possible reality where the temperature may raise to way over 150 degrees or more and would certainly be our downfall.

Mother nature, God or whatever energy causes these spectacular displays of power certainly and obviously has no sympathy or interest in preserving mankind for their "so needed" future when these changes occur. This time, it's mostly our fault and consequently, our responsibility to offset this oncoming geological and atmospheric heat spell. If we don't, then we must prepare to either fry, steam or boil alive. No human, animal or above the ground creature will escape it.

If anyone from outer space does land on Earth later, there will be plenty of evidence on "this" planet of how mankind destroyed himself and most other living things too.

Sure, we've had a lot of rain around the world lately directly because of the icebergs melting, but when they have finished melting, that type of downpour will stop. After that, the dry heat will bake any fresh water dry to where we never imagined.

All influences and energies must stay focused on the project. Good luck to us all. There will be more updated information on this subject as they become available to the public. Watch for the new issue as it becomes published.

Your author, Lloyd E. McIlveen unveils a chronological list of many and various book subjects presenting controversial, educational, uplifting, futuristic, self-helping, philosophical, psychological, entertaining and other stimulating concepts of which are and will be displayed with brief descriptions of each book as follows:

1. "Evaluating Outdated Beliefs" This is a report, viewed through the perception of your author of the evolutionary process and changes occurring in belief; especially in the area of religion and spirituality, This was designed for the benefit of broadening individual perception, perspective and viewing "another" plane of belief while revealing fallacies in theological indoctrination. This is an improved revision of the book's origin.

2. "Staying Alive On Planet Earth I" This is a psychology of health required to stabilize and

maintain better health for the benefit of living a much longer life. Source: A lifetime of study, problems, recoveries and many successes more in natural methods.

3. "Understanding Loss To Relieve The Anguish" Loss of anything involves many distractions and disrupting emotional disarray. Gaining greater understanding of these emotions offsets the misery of them and enhances optimism of confidence and support for emotional weakness before, at and during the time of loss.

4. "Understanding Preventing And Eliminating Cancer" presents new views on the wonders of natural methods for practical use.

5. "Paradox Of Progress Unfolding I" This is a tale told by a man "many" centuries into the future about an exciting, overwhelming and terrifying occurrence on planet Earth as a result of their wondrous progress around the time of 2300

A.D. Hang onto your seats! #2 is a second issue later on the list.

6. "Offsetting Climate Change And Nuclear Waste Contamination" This view of the two exposes the hazards, inevitabilities and possible solutions needed now for preventing a "too late" disaster that will affect all living beings too soon.

7. "What God Is And Is Not" This is a study of spiritual possibilities designed, not particularly to remold conventional mannerisms of belief, but to open and expand perception in the most controversial subject of mankind; the subject of God and whether mankind will or won't expand that consciousness along with all progress and growth on Earth and in the universe.

8. "Kids Of The Crick" This is a story of four old fashioned country kids setting out on a weekend adventure in their countryside of tall grass, mountains, rivers, animals, caves and strange

living beings. Sometimes, they aren't sure whether it's all real or not.

9. "Paradox Of Destiny Explained" eliminates the mysteries, facades, fantasies and deceptions of how, where, way and when we do what we do and opens new possibilities for expanding our beliefs and consciousness pertaining to this study of available options that may influence insight for growth, change or even justify present mannerisms of what may control the individual, planet Earth or the whole universe and is not zealous, fanatic or bigoted; only assertively revealing.

10. "Paradox Of Progress Unfolding 2" This book is a continued fiction story and can be considered exemplary of "major" human changes that alienated millions of people to another planet in the future. They are led by the elements of unexpected surprises of which is par for the course with gutsy space

pioneers. The first "Paradox Of Progress Unfolding I" must be read first to understand and appreciate the disproportional attitudes and positions of people on a threshold of major change and disasters upon them. This is not only a tale of travel, trials and tribulations, it is philosophically stimulating and adds toward future insightful expansion of the human species.

11. "Staying Alive On Planet Earth 2" This is an extended version of the original psychology of health for living a longer life. More knowledge allows more life.

12. "Preventing The Doom Of Mankind" This is a stimulating, vitalizing and somewhat shocking description of how mankind is "truly" faced with extinction in the "near" future due to their own faults of progress. It's very educational and needed now to help offset that inevitability where the odds dictate we will all perish if we

don't adhere to this offsetting of which "is" possible to achieve.

13. "Spiritual Transformation Of The Fourth Millennium" Old-time conventional religion is fading. New-time spirituality is on the rise. Objective realism is the prime issue here for future inclined thinking and believing.

14. "Understanding The Science Of Creative Mind" This is a study for discovering, developing and practicing a psychological powerhouse within for conquering the unconquerable, achieving the impossible or doing things no one has done all depending on, of course, the makeup and determination of the individual. This study brings out a greater potential of the individual's abilities when taken seriously. This was compiled from a lifetime of study and experience from your author.

15. "Living to 150" is a guidance program for intentions of anyone desiring a longer than longer life which is insightfully and innovatively educational for that purpose.

16. "The Act Of Getting One's Act Together" If anyone, business or nation wants to develop their stance, priorities and position in life, this is a chance for them to get their act together more than ever.

17. "Making Changes From This Point Forward" The design of this book is for the purpose of preventing repeated mistakes of unforeseen surprises due to what we weren't or aren't aware of that did, can or will happen again. It's all about gaining or rearranging change consciousness in this area.

18. "Relationships For All" This is a carefully arranged view of how relationships can function much better when initiated or guided by the experiences of many experts and your author

who have had failures and successes in their very human encounters. The experiences of more relationships result in wiser judgments and approaches to others.

19. "The We Between Us" helps us in discovering who is good for us and who is not. First it is a study in the book. Then it is a study with people of what exists in two party's minds (individuals business or nations) when first confronted. A real time saver in evaluating possible compatibility or not between the two for anyone. It works.

20. "Passion Of Dance" This is a narrative on progress, value and guidance for the dance inclined. It's informative and inspiring with its history and recent magnetism.

21. "Open That Door" to love. This book is comprehensively all about love. It's not a storybook. It clears up the differences of love

that causes misunderstanding, suspicion and deception.

22. "Get The Spirit" This book describes controversial and somewhat intertwined conventional views of spirit, spirits and spirituality. This book untangles the "usual" views and presents a more perspective manner of living with these concepts of mind.

23. "Stories Of What They Couldn't Or Wouldn't Tell" Ages are from babies to 100 years; twenty four of them.

24. "Improving On Love And Relationships" This one is two books in one. Part one "Open That Door" is a psychology of love that enhances perspective to understand and adapt to a very popular, but deceiving, repressed and ignored emotion; love. Part two covers "Relationships For All" which elaborates on origination, different types, significance, deceptions, desires, experiences,

communication, possibilities, future and guidance of relationships. It's comprehensive and also derived from a lifetime of relationship experiences and serious study.

Notes

Notes

Notes

Notes

Notes